YOUR KNOWLEDGE HAS VALUE

Isabel Mund

"E Pluribus Unum?" – Still Valid for Everyone?

A Discussion about the Possibilities of Hispanic-Americans to Live the American Dream in 21st-century America

GRIN Verlag

Bibliografische Information der Deutschen Nationalbibliothek:

Die Deutsche Bibliothek verzeichnet diese Publikation in der Deutschen National-
bibliografie; detaillierte bibliografische Daten sind im Internet über http://dnb.d-
nb.de/ abrufbar.

Imprint:

Copyright © 2013 GRIN Verlag GmbH
Druck und Bindung: Books on Demand GmbH, Norderstedt Germany
ISBN: 978-3-656-50412-2

This book at GRIN:

http://www.grin.com/en/e-book/233368/e-pluribus-unum-still-valid-for-everyone

ersity of Malta

lty of Arts

rtment of English

y-Unit: ENG3083 American Studies: An Introduction

"E Pluribus Unum?" – Still Valid for Everyone? –

Discussion about the Possibilities of Hispanic-Americans to Live the American Dream in 21st-century America

ded in by:

ne: Isabel Mund

al number of words: 2482

e of submission: 10th June 2013

'American dream *n*. (also American Dream) (with *the*) the ideal that every citizen of the United States should have an equal opportunity to achieve success and prosperity through hard work, determination, and initiative'[1].   ----- Oxford English Dictionary

The concept of the American Dream is as old as the American society itself. During the history of the United States of America this fundamental concept and its interpretation have changed a lot. It all started in the 1880s. During the ages of the American expansion towards the West[2] the American Dream was reflected in the possibility of a person to start a completely new life, for example by setting up a farm on his or her own[3]. After the Second World War this interpretation of the American Dream changed not only because the whole territory of the North-American continent has been conquered until then. The more influential factor was the huge impact that the Industrialisation and Modernisation had on the American society from the beginning of the 20th century onwards. In fact, a steady economic growth combined with the need for more workers which was compensated by an increasing immigration particularly from Europe led to a new and self-confident way of thinking about the U.S. [4]. This interpretation of the American Dream intensified after the Second World War and can be summarised as involving a desire 'to move to the suburbs and [to have] the ability to own a home, raise a family, send one's children to college, and support oneself in old age'[5]. Apart from the fact that there are a lot of different ways of understanding the American Dream, the most common interpretation is that of economic success possible for every American. And even nowadays the American Dream is based on the notion that if an American works hard, he or she can achieve a good life. This concept includes two very important elements. At first, it is based on the assumption that a person can reach his or her aims without being limited by structures or other factors like age, sex or even race. Therefore, individual success only depends on the amount of engagement everyone is willing to give. This notion is linked to the second element the American Dream includes. The concept of 'everything is possible as long you work hard enough for it' includes the assumption that every American is able to have success. Hence, the concept of the American Dream embraces everyone living in the United States of America. Can that be true? Is the American Dream really an all-embracing vision?

---

[1] Taken from Oxford English Dictionary, retrieved from http://www.oed.com.ejournals.um.edu.mt/view/Entry/6342 (accessed 25.05.2013).
[2] Horst Dippel, *Geschichte der USA* (München: C. H. Beck, 2010), p. 41-43.
[3] Brian Starks, 'The New Economy and the American Dream: Examining the Effect of Work Conditions on Beliefs about Economic Opportunity', *The Sociological Quarterly*, 44 (2003), pp. 205-225 (p. 206).
[4] Dippel, p. 44-45.
[5] Starks, pp. 205-225 (p. 206).

If the answer is yes – how can it be possible that nearly 47 million[6] Americans are living close to or even below the poverty line? Furthermore, if there is something like the 'Unamerican Dream', which is particularly described by Alfred Hornung[7], it cannot be true that every American can have access to this concept. What about the minorities in the American society? Some statistics and surveys show that in particular minorities are part of that group including the most poor and unemployed people in the American society. If that is true, how can one explain this phenomenon? In this essay I want to focus on a specific minority group in the American society, namely the Hispanics. By using them as an example, the possibility of this group to live the American Dream is going to be discussed. While doing this, I am going to concentrate on and discuss three aspects which are linked to the access to the American Dream. The first one is referring to the position that Hispanics have in the American society. Connected with this aspect is the second one which deals with the preconditions every Hispanic has access to. In this case I will focus on education because this factor provides the background for every further success in life. If there is a lack in education, there cannot be economical success. The last point I want to discuss is the very important question: Are there some Hispanics who are already living the American Dream? And if yes, are they just exceptions or is there indeed an increasing number of people gaining access to success?

The Hispanics – also called 'Latinos'[8] in some papers and surveys – are the largest minority group in the USA. The official U.S. Census of 2010 reported nearly 50 million Hispanics living in the United States, predominantly living in Puerto Rico, Texas and California[9]. According to a survey of the U.S. Census Bureau one can 'define' a Hispanic as 'a person of Cuban, Mexican, Puerto Rican, South or Central American, or other Spanish culture or origin regardless of race'[10]. Most of them are immigrants or at least children of former immigrants, predominately coming from Puerto Rico or Mexico. Apart from the fact that nearly all of the Hispanics speak rather Spanish than English[11] at home it seems – according to a survey from 2004 – that Hispanics have a good position in the American society. This report showed that

---

[6] Carmen DeNavas-Walt, Bernadette D. Proctor, and Jessica C. Smith, *Income, Poverty, and Health Insurance Coverage in the United States: 2011* (Washington, DC: U.S. Government Printing Office, 2012), p.13.
[7] In this essay Hornung describes the existence of more than one American Dream which is, in his opinion, only accessible to the so-called WASP-Americans. Foreigners are said to create their own version of the American Dream so that there are a lot of different 'Un-American Dreams'. See Alfred Hornung, 'The Un-American Dream', *Amerikastudien / American Studies*, 44 (1999), pp. 545-553.
[8] Karen R. Humes, Nicholas A. Jones, and Roberto R. Ramirez, *Overview of Race and Hispanic Origin: 2010* (Washington, DC: U.S. Government Printing Office, 2010), p. 2.
[9] Ibid., p. 18.
[10] Ibid., p.2.
[11] Roberto R. Ramirez, *We the People: Hispanics in the United States*, (Washington, DC: U.S. Government Printing Office, 2004), p.10.

the Hispanics are taking part in labour force and that they share some cultural customs like living in a household as a married couple[12]. Even in terms of education there is not a huge gap between the total population and the Hispanic minority. In fact, the survey showed that almost ten per cent of the Hispanics are able to get at least a bachelor's degree[13]. Furthermore, the survey showed that approximately 15 per cent of all men and nearly 23 per cent of all women with Hispanic origin are in a higher position like for example the management[14]. Therefore, it seems that Hispanics of course take part in American society and since they do so, they must have access to the American Dream as well. On the other hand, when taking a deeper look, one can observe a lot of differences between the Hispanics and other groups. By analysing the given data, one can identify some slight differences with regard to education between the part of Hispanics having a higher profession and the total population. In contrast to the data mentioned above, nearly 32 per cent of all men or 36 per cent of all women in the U.S. are in a higher profession[15]. In addition to that, there are significant differences in the educational level of the total population in comparison to that of the Hispanics. While only 51 per cent of the Hispanics have a high-school diploma, more than 80 per cent of the whole population passed this level of education[16]. Moreover, only ten per cent of all Hispanics older than 25 years have a bachelor's degree, whereas nearly 25 per cent of the whole American population were able to reach this kind of qualification[17]. Some studies on that give a good explanation of this phenomenon. Susan B. Neuman, a professor of Educational Studies at Philadelphia University, found out that there is a close connection between poverty and educational success. In her study she analysed and compared two different neighbourhoods of Philadelphia with regard to the access that children from this region have to educational resources like schools, libraries etc.. The results are clear. Whereas the children from the financially well-situated neighbourhood, which was predominantly populated by white Americans, had a good access to a huge amount of resources having a good quality, children from the other neighbourhood, which was populated by a lot of minorities and particularly Hispanics, did not. Furthermore, Neuman pointed out that '[h]igh-income families now spend nearly 7 times as much on their children's development as low-income families do'[18]. In fact, Hispanics belong to a group in American society which shows the biggest percentage of poor people. Therefore, one can

---

[12] Ramirez, p. 7.
[13] Ibid., p. 11.
[14] Ibid., p. 13.
[15] Ramirez, p. 13.
[16] Ibid., p. 11.
[17] Ibid., p. 11.
[18] Susan B. Neuman, 'The American Dream: Slipping away?', *Educational Leadership*, 70 (2013), pp. 18-22 (p. 20).

conclude that Hispanics tend to live in such neighbourhoods having a negative influence on the education of their children and therefore, they are not as educated as other social groups. This can be used as an explanation for the data given above as well as for the assumption that Hispanics do not have the same access to jobs which are based on a higher educational level. Hence, Hispanics do not have the same possibility to get access to fulfil their American Dream that the other groups of the society have.

This fact is linked to some other factors. For example, some data particularly given in the survey presented above pointed out that nearly 40 per cent of the Hispanics are immigrants1[19]. Obviously, it is much harder for them to find a job or to get access to important resources. These people are forced to live in neighbourhoods which have a negative effect on education. If they are workers they are limited to jobs which give them a low income. This can be proved by some statistical figures. In 2011 the medium income of members of the Hispanic group was 38.264$ a year whereas the medium income in America was 50.025$ per year[20]. This does not only evoke a vicious circle of low income, bad neighbourhood and little education, but it also has some psychological results. As shown by Brian Starks, Hispanics as well as other minorities in America do not believe in the American Dream as much as the white Americans do[21]. The reasons for that are of course the bad perspectives that a lot of Hispanics have.

It would be wrong to draw a negative picture just including black and white – or in this case being able to live the American Dream or not. Naturally, there is always an in-between. Of course, as shown in above, there are some differences and disadvantages for the Hispanics but on the other hand there are of course some reasons why one could say that the American Dream still exists for the Hispanics as well.

Firstly, although Hispanics are among these social groups having a high rate of poverty, they are not the poorest social group in the United States of America. With regard to the statistical data the Black Americans or African Americans are the poorest members of the American society. Nearly 25 per cent of all African Americans are below the poverty line whereas only 23 per cent of all Hispanics are affected by poverty[22]. The poorest social groups in America are the American Indian and Alaska native people with approximately 27 per cent of people

---

[19] Ramirez, p.8.
[20] Ibid., p. 15.
[21] Starks, pp. 205-225 (p. 207).
[22] Ramirez, p.16.

below the poverty line[23]. Furthermore, even the white Americans, which are said to be the social group having the most economic success, are affected by poverty. In fact, there are approximately 25 million white Americans living in poverty[24]. Hence, being poor is not only a phenomenon of minority groups but rather for every social group in America, including specific consequences.

Secondly, there is not only an increasing number of Hispanics in general but particularly of successful Hispanics. This can be observed when studying the income of the Hispanics. The income of Hispanics increased a lot. Between 1999 and 2011 the average income of the Hispanic population grew from 34.000$ a year up to 38.624$ per year[25]. The average income of all American households kept on a same level by nearly 50.000$[26]. An increasing income is a good marker for higher qualification as well as for success. Furthermore, the amount of Hispanics working in high professions particularly as merchants for little companies is still increasing[27]. Moreover, the numbers given in surveys are a good basis for politics in order to improve the situation of the Hispanics. Hence, there are a lot of governmental programs supporting the Hispanics in their private life as well as on an educational level, namely for example the Hispanic College Fund, Hispanic Scholarship Fund or a Family Fund for the support of young parents[28]. All these governmental programs are providing money as well as the imparting of special offers, contacts and further support. By this the government aims to enable the Hispanics to get access to the American Dream.

How can all these facts be concluded? As shown in the first part of the essay, the Hispanic minority in the United States takes part in the society. Of course, the Hispanics are part of the everyday life in America, particularly in the States in which their population is concentrated. Hispanics have to work in order to support their families, they have to go to school and they are taking part in the cultural life. But are they able to live the American Dream like a 'typical' American? The figures given in the first part of the essay show a dark picture. It was proved that the Hispanics have a lot of disadvantages in American society. They are poorer then a white American, their average income is nearly 12.000$ less than the national one and they have to suffer from the consequences caused by this. This means in particular that His-

---

[23] Alemayehu Bishaw, Kayla Fontenot, and Suzanne Macartney, *Poverty Rates for Selected Detailed Race and Hispanic Groups by State and Place: 2007–2011* (Washington, DC: U.S. Government Printing Office, 2011), p. 2.
[24] According to the data provided in Bishaw, Fontenot, and Macartney, p.2.
[25] See Ramirez, p.14 and DeNavas-Walt, Proctor, and Smith, p.5.
[26] DeNavas-Walt, Proctor, and Smith, p.5.
[27] Ramirez, p.13.
[28] http://www.hsf.net/Scholarship-Programs.aspx (accessed 09.06.2013)

panics more often have to live in bad neighbourhoods which provide a bad environment for a good education of children. Because of that one can observe that Hispanic children have not as much success in school or even in University as other social groups. And this is the reason why they can neither reach a good educational level or degree nor a profession in a higher position. This leads to the assumption that Hispanics have a smaller possibility to have success than other social groups in America. On the other hand, Hispanics are sharing their situation with all of the other social groups in America. Even the white majority is affected by poverty and its consequences and with the American and Alaskan Indians as well as with the Black Americans there are two other minorities having a higher poverty rate than the Hispanics. Moreover, particularly because of some governmental programs the situation of this special social group is improving at the moment. Supported by a lot of governmental funds the number of Hispanic students will increase in the next years. Furthermore, some developments in the past led to a growth of the income of Hispanic workers. This fact makes optimistic that during the next years more and more Latinos will have access to the American Dream. In fact, because of the development shown in this essay, the number of Hispanics being able to live a good life increased so that in some years the differences between the social groups will become smaller and smaller.

One can conclude that the American Dream, particularly in the economic sense of the term, is still a very powerful concept in the American society. The Hispanic minority as a growing social group in America has only limited access to live this concept and to get a huge economic success. Because of governmental programs, a changing income-situation and maybe because of a changing attitude towards this concept the amount of Hispanics living the American Dream will increase and the stereotype of the poor Hispanic being unsuccessful and disillusioned will disappear.

List of Works Cited

Bishaw, Alemayehu, Fontenot, Kayla, and Suzanne Macartney, *Poverty Rates for Selected Detailed Race and Hispanic Groups by State and Place: 2007–2011* (Washington, DC: U.S. Government Printing Office, 2011)

DeNavas-Walt, Carmen, Proctor, Bernadette D., and Jessica C. Smith, *Income, Poverty, and Health Insurance Coverage in the United States: 2011* (Washington, DC: U.S. Government Printing Office, 2012)

Dippel, Horst, *Geschichte der USA* (München: C. H. Beck, 2010)

Hornung, Alfred, 'The Un-American Dream', *Amerikastudien / American Studies*, 44 (1999), pp. 545-553

Humes, Karen R., Jones, Nicholas A., and Roberto R. Ramirez, *Overview of Race and Hispanic Origin: 2010* (Washington, DC: U.S. Government Printing Office, 2010)

Neuman, Susan B., 'The American Dream: Slipping away?', *Educational Leadership*, 70 (2013), pp. 18-22

Ramirez, Roberto R., *We the People: Hispanics in the United States*, (Washington, DC: U.S. Government Printing Office, 2004)

Starks, Brian, 'The New Economy and the American Dream: Examining the Effect of Work Conditions on Beliefs about Economic Opportunity', *The Sociological Quarterly*, 44 (2003), pp. 205-225

http://www.hsf.net/Scholarship-Programs.aspx (accessed 09.06.2013)

http://www.oed.com.ejournals.um.edu.mt/view/ Entry/6342 (accessed 25.05.2013)